A

# SUBSTITUTE

FOR

SIR J. CAMPBELL'S SUMMARY LAW

FOR OBTAINING JUDGMENTS ON

## BONDS, BILLS, AND NOTES,

APPLICABLE TO ALL OTHER DEBTS, AS WELL AS DEBTS
ON THOSE SECURITIES.

### BY AN ATTORNEY.

> Daily experience proves that the time which the defendant really requires to prepare an honest defence, will be anxiously sought by the distressed debtor, who has no defence, to put off the day of payment: for this purpose he avails himself of every expedient which the practice of the court allows to obtain delay. Unhappily he attains his object at present, very often by a sacrifice of his own means, as well as those which the humanity of his friends will supply, in many cases sufficient to have paid the original demand; nor is this the only grievance, the expences of the plaintiff are in the mean time increasing in the same ratio, till at last he finds he has incurred as much expence as his original demand, in many cases a great deal more, to make his debtor insolvent.—*Sir James Scarlett's Letter to the Common Law Commissioners. First Report.*

LONDON:
H. DIXON, CAREY STREET, LINCOLN'S INN.
1835.
*Price, One Shilling.*

In the interest of creating a more extensive selection of rare historical book reprints, we have chosen to reproduce this title even though it may possibly have occasional imperfections such as missing and blurred pages, missing text, poor pictures, markings, dark backgrounds and other reproduction issues beyond our control. Because this work is culturally important, we have made it available as a part of our commitment to protecting, preserving and promoting the world's literature. Thank you for your understanding.

# INTRODUCTION

Bonds, Bills, and Promissory Notes are so strong *primâ facie* evidences of Debt, and the right of the Creditor on them is so rarely questionable, that a summary method of obtaining judgments at Law upon those securities has now been recommended to the Legislature.

According to the present practice of the Courts, if an acceptor of a bill deny the debt by a plea, the plaintiff must resort to a trial by a jury with the attendant expences of counsel, attorney, witnesses, and court fees, to prove a liability which admits of no dispute. The defendant is not required to *guarantee* in any way the truth of his plea, and that which is so styled consists of a few words written on half a sheet of paper, which is left at the office of the plaintiff's attorney, and is the *only one proceeding* the defendant need take to throw on the plaintiff the expences of a nisi prius trial.

The want of such a *guarantee* from a resisting defendant is an evil which Sir John Campbell's bill proposes to remedy as to bonds and negotiable securities, by requiring from the defendant, within ten days after the service of the process, a full security for debt and costs, and in default of it, judgment is given for the plaintiff. But this plan suggests two objections; first, that the requiring security in so summary a way may work much hardship and injustice; and secondly, that the facilitating the recovery of only one description of debt is but a partial amendment, for the evil referred to will still affect all the book debts, and other simple contract debts of traders and retailers for which written securities have not been given, and which latter class far exceeds the former in number.

An efficient remedy should meet both descriptions of debt; and that the evil is not a partial but a universal one is seen in this, that every tradesman in the country is impressed with the idea of the danger of suing for debts, and many will lose them rather than venture into law. These people, when they clamour for local courts, mistake their wants; they require a means of recovering cheaply and without risk of adding much to their loss, undisputed debts, which need no judicial inquiry or proof. The returns to parliament would shew (what an attorney's experience tells him) that at the least, nine actions out of ten, in the superior courts, are for debts of this kind. Now a trial before a jury, whether of twelve men or six, is a cumbersome and costly apparatus to get in such debts, and the great object therefore is to prevent defendants pleading in these cases by giving them motives to refrain from it, and if a plan could be found to effect this, the popular cry for local courts would be no longer heard, particularly now that issues of small amount can be sent to the sheriff to determine, and that new rules of pleading are reducing the expences of *bonâ fide* litigation to the lowest point consistent with sound judicial investigation.

The scheme contained in the following pages has for its object the prevention of this groundless and vexatious resistance to actions for undisputed debts, by compelling a debtor in the first instance to consider the claim made on him and his own circumstances—by taking away all necessity and excuse for a groundless plea—by making such a plea more clearly and tangibly a breach of moral duty—by giving the honest debtor an opportunity to render his means available—by punishing the man who inexcusably shall have defended a just action, and wilfully increased his creditor's loss, and by these means affording to the creditor a *guarantee* in suing for his debts, and to the debtor a protection against an oppressive creditor or attorney.

If it *would* accomplish these ends, there would be no occasion to invade the uniformity of actions by introducing the Scotch law of bills of exchange; and many of the purposes of the local courts would be answered by it: it is extremely simple, and would not cause confusion in practice—it makes no new offices, and requires no compensation—it extends to debts of every amount—it would give an advantage to actions by serviceable process, which might reconcile commercial men to the abolition of the law of arrest; and, though it might reduce the common law profits of attorneys (a consideration not to be disregarded by the public, who are deeply interested in the respectability of the profession), it would place those profits on a wholesome footing; and, if it rendered the local courts unnecessary, would save the profession from the brood of pettifoggers which that system would bring into existence.

Some will object to the plan of giving the debtor, upon his confessing the debt, a month's time for payment; but be it observed that a judgment cannot now be obtained sooner; and the quick succession of declaration, plea, issue, and notice of trial, to which a debtor, wishing for time, must now submit, frequently disables him from paying any thing: and if it be said that the fear of these expences will make a debtor pay more promptly, the answer is, that where there is ability to save expence, the debt would be safe at the end of the month, whilst in the case of a man without present means, the advantage both to debtor and creditor, of arresting the course of the costs, is too obvious to enlarge upon.

Professional readers will immediately discover the economy of saving altogether the declaration, even where judgment is entered up.

The plan does not disturb the present practice where the debt is in dispute; actions for debt are, at their commencement, subjected to a test, which sifts the defendable from the defenceless ones, provides for the latter by economising their expence, and lets the former pass through to proceed as heretofore.

With regard to the punishment for vexatiously pleading: the insolvent court at the present time imprisons for this offence, but so many innocent men are *forced* to plead, that it is not considered a moral delinquency, and under the existing practice it is difficult to find out where the *crimen* begins. Under the bankrupt law there is no punishment for wilful pleas, and therefore bankrupts escape. The present scheme clearly defines the offence in question, and proposes a punishment as the condition of receiving relief by insolvency or bankruptcy from the pressure of debts. This punishment may be modified according to the laws hereafter to give that relief.

THE

# DRAFT OF AN ACT

FOR

FACILITATING THE RECOVERY OF DEBTS.

---

I. WHEREAS, according to the present practice of the courts of law at Westminster, creditors suing for just debts are delayed and put to great expence by debtors vexatiously defending the actions brought against them; wherefore, for remedy thereof, &c. &c.

II. THAT every writ of summons issuing from the courts of law at Westminster, as the commencement of any action for the recovery of any debt, shall be in the form marked No. 1, in the Schedule to this Act, having the notice or warning in the said form specified thereto subjoined, and *on the service of such writ, the defendant shall likewise be served with a detailed particular of the demand* for which such action is brought.

III. THAT *within ten days after service* of such writ of summons and particular of demand, or within eight days from the service of the demand of appearance hereinafter mentioned, inclusive of the days of service, *the defendant shall, if he* purpose to *defend* such action, *enter an appearance* to such writ of summons with the proper officer for receiving the appearance thereon; *and at the same time* shall *file* with such officer *a declaration*, signed by him the said defendant, *that he believes that he hath good ground of defence* to the action on the merits, which declaration shall be styled, " An Averment of Merits," and shall be in the form No. 3, of the Schedule to this Act; and the signature of the defendant to such declaration or averment shall be witnessed by an attorney of one of the courts of Westminster, and an affidavit of such signature and attestation shall be filed with such averment.

IV. THAT where it shall be made to appear to one of the judges of the courts of Westminster to be necessary or reasonable that such averment of merits should be signed by the attorney of the defendant for and on his behalf, then such judge shall so order; and the averment so signed (the signature thereto being verified by affidavit) shall be sufficient for all the purposes of this Act; and so likewise if the plaintiff's attorney or agent shall consent to the defendant's attorney signing such averment for and on behalf of the defendant, then, upon the plaintiff's attorney or agent signing his consent under the averment, the averment so signed (the signatures thereto being verified by affidavit) shall be sufficient for all the purposes of this Act.

V. THAT no appearance entered by any defendant to any writ of summons issued under the authority of this Act shall be deemed a sufficient appearance, without an averment of merits being filed therewith (except in case of the notice of plea in abatement hereinafter mentioned), unless the plaintiff, or his attorney, shall consent in writing to waive the filing of the averment of merits by all or any of the defendants; or unless a judge, upon sufficient cause shown, shall order that the same be not filed, then and in such case such non-averment shall not affect the regularity of the proceedings in the cause.

VI. THAT if it shall be made to appear to one of the judges of the said courts, that farther and better particulars of the plaintiff's demand should be given, or that farther time for appearing and filing the averment of merits should be granted, then it shall be lawful for such judge to make such orders therein as he shall see fit.

VII. THAT *if within the time allowed, an appearance* and averment of merits *be not filed, the plaintiff shall cause to be served upon the defendant,* either personally, or by leaving the same at his usual residence, or last place of abode, *a demand of appearance and averment,* requiring such appearance and averment to be entered *within eight days* from the service thereof, which demand shall be in the form marked No. 2, in the Schedule to this Act.

VIII. THAT if an appearance and averment be not entered pursuant to such demand thereof as aforesaid, the *defendant shall be deemed to have confessed the debt,* and the plaintiff shall be at liberty to enter the proceedings on *a roll of the court, in the form No. 6 of the Schedule* to this Act, and to tax the costs of the action, and *the officer with whom such appearance and averment should,* according to this Act, *have been filed,* upon affidavit of the personal service of the writ of summons and particulars of demand, and of the due service of the demand of appearance (with the writ of summons, a copy of the particulars of demand, and a copy of the demand of appearance thereto annexed), being filed with him, *shall if such services shall appear to him to have been regularly made,* and such costs duly taxed, *certify on such roll that execution may issue* for such debt and costs, and the *plaintiff may then carry such roll to the signer of the writs of execution of the proper court, who shall* thereupon *sign the writ of execution, keeping the said roll,* and if required by the plaintiff, or his attorney, receiving also a minute or præcipe for docketing thereof: and the said signer of the writs of execution shall, from time to time, deliver over the rolls, and the minutes or præcipes of docket, to the clerk of the judgments of the court, who shall forthwith docket the judgments.

IX. THAT in case it shall be made to appear by affidavit to the satisfaction of the court out of which the aforesaid writ of summons issued, or if in vacation, of any judge of either of the said courts, that any defendant has not been personally served with any such writ of summons as hereinbefore mentioned, and has not according to the exigency thereof appeared to the action, and cannot be compelled so to do without some more efficacious process, then if it shall be shewn to such court or judge, that a copy of the writ of summons, and a detailed particular of demand for which the action is brought, has been left at the defendant's dwelling-house, or otherwise sufficiently served to the satisfaction of the court or judge, then and in any such case, it shall be lawful for such court or judge to order *a writ of distringas* to be issued, directed to the sheriff of the county wherein the dwelling-house or place of abode of such defendant shall be situate, or to the sheriff of any other county, or to any officer to be named by such court or judge, in order *to compel the appearance* of such defendant, which writ of distringas shall be in the form and with the notice subscribed thereto mentioned in the Schedule to this Act marked No. 5, which writ of distringas and notice, or a copy thereof, shall be served on such defendant if he can be met with: or if not, shall be left at the place where such distringas shall be executed, and a true copy of every such writ and notice shall be delivered, together therewith to the sheriff, or other officer to whom such writ shall be directed; and every such writ shall be made returnable on some day in term, not being less than fifteen days after the teste thereof, and shall bear teste on the day of the issuing thereof, whether in term or in vacation; and if such writ of distringas shall be returned *non est inventus*, and *nulla bona*, and any defendant against whom such writ of distringas issued, shall not appear and file the averment of merits within eight days inclusive, after the return thereof, and it shall be made to appear by affidavit to the satisfaction of the court out of which such writ of distringas issued, or in vacation, of any judge of either of the said courts, that due and proper means were taken and used to serve and execute such writ of distringas, and also that the plaintiff has a good subsisting debt, then it shall be lawful for such court or judge to authorize the plaintiff, upon giving such further notice to the defendant, and in such manner as the court or judge shall direct; or, if so ordered, without further notice to enter the proceedings on a judgment roll, in the form No. 8 of the Schedule to this Act, and to issue execution thereon forthwith, or if the court or judge shall not think fit to order judgment and execution, then it shall be lawful for such court or judge to authorize the party suing out such writ to enter an appearance for such defendant, and to proceed thereon to judgment according to the practice of the court in cases not within the authority of this Act.

X. THAT *the defendant* having been served with process in manner hereinbefore mentioned, *shall be at liberty* within the time by this Act allowed for his appearing and averring merits, in case such time shall expire sooner than thirty-one days inclusive from the service of the writ, *to file* with the officer with whom the appearance to such process would have been entered, a *confession of the debt, and a submission to pay the same, together with the costs claimed, at the expiration of thirty-one days from the service of the writ of summons*, including the day of such service, or of any less number of days;

*and thereupon the plaintiff shall stay all proceedings*, until the period so limited for payment shall have elapsed, when if the defendant shall not have satisfied the debt and costs confessed, the plaintiff shall be at liberty to enter the proceedings on a roll of the court, in the form No. 7, of the Schedule hereto; and the officer with whom such confession shall have been filed, shall certify on the roll that execution may issue for the debt and costs confessed, together with such costs for the judgment, as by any rule or order of the said courts shall, from time to time, in such case be fixed, and execution thereupon shall issue, and the judgment roll be carried in, in the manner provided by the 8th Section of this Act. Provided always, that where such confession shall be filed after the expiration of the ten days allowed for appearance, and before demand of appearance served, and only the costs claimed by the writ shall be confessed, the plaintiff shall be at liberty to refer any farther costs to be taxed by the Master, and the same, when so taxed, shall be recoverable, under the said confession.

XI. THAT after a defendant shall have filed a confession of the debt, in manner hereinbefore mentioned, *it shall be lawful for any one of the Judges* of the said courts, if any sufficient cause can be shewn, to order *such further stay of proceedings* beyond the expiration of the time of payment limited by such confession, as in such case shall be reasonable; and if, after the filing of such confession as aforesaid, the plaintiff shall shew, to the satisfaction of any one of such judges, that *the delay of execution* till the time it might on such confession be obtained, *would*, by reason of the defendant meditating flight or a fraudulent removal of his assets, *endanger the plaintiff's debt;* then *it shall be lawful for such judge*, if he think fit, *to order* the judgment to be entered, and *execution to issue* thereon forthwith, any thing in this Act, or in such confession contained to the contrary notwithstanding.

XII. THAT the aforesaid confession of debt shall be in the form marked No. 4, in the Schedule to this Act, and shall be signed by the defendant, and shall be witnessed by his attorney, or by any other attorney of any of the courts of Westminster, acting therein as the agent of the defendant's attorney, and such signatures and attestations shall be verified by an affidavit to be thereunto annexed, and filed therewith, and no appearance by the defendant shall be requisite to give effect to such confession.

XIII. THAT *after an appearance* shall have been entered, *with an averment of merits, the action shall proceed according to the present forms and practice,* or other the forms and practice for the time being of the court in which such action shall be pending; *provided nevertheless,* that if the defendant, or there being two or more defendants, any one or more of them, shall suffer judgment by default of pleading, or shall make default in appearing on the hearing or trial of any issue raised by him or them in law or fact; or if, on the defendant or defendants appearing upon the hearing or trial of any such issue, the judge or court shall certify that the filing of the averment by such defendant or defendants, or any one or more of them, was vexatious, and without reasonable and probable cause, then the plaintiff shall be at liberty to cause judgment to be entered up against such defendant or defendants, in case of default, with a suggestion on the roll of such default made after an averment of merits; or in case of such certificate granted by the judge or court on the hearing or trial of such issue as aforesaid, with a suggestion of such certificate; and be it enacted, *that where* by any such judgment by default or the aforesaid certificate of a court or judge, or by other satisfactory evidence, *it shall appear that the averment of merits was filed vexatiously, and without reasonable and probable cause, and the person* who shall in such manner have averred merits, *shall apply for the benefit of any Act for the relief of insolvent persons, such person shall not have* or be allowed *the benefit of such Act, until he shall* have *submitted to such sentence of imprisonment as the court* or commissioner to whom such application shall be made upon such proof, as aforesaid, tendered by any creditor or creditors of such person, *shall think fit to adjudge,* and which such court or commissioner is hereby empowered and required to adjudge, so as the same shall not exceed     months, nor be less than one month, for each offence; and farther, that *where any person shall* in like manner *have averred merits vexatiously,* and without reasonable and probable cause, *and shall become bankrupt,* and shall apply to any commissioner or commissioners, acting under the authority of any act now or hereafter to be in force concerning bankrupts, for the signing by such commissioner or commissioners of the certificate of discharge of such bankrupt under the fiat against him, *such commissioner* or *commissioners shall on sufficient proof of such vexatious averment* tendered by any creditor or creditors of such person, and whether the parties, against whom the vexatious defence shall have been made, have or have not proved their debt or debts under the fiat, *postpone the signing of such certificate until the expiration of such period of time as to him or them shall seem fit;* so as such period shall not exceed the term of     years, nor be less than     months, from the time of such commissioner or commissioners awarding such postponement: and in case the certificate of any such bankrupt shall have been signed by the commissioner or commissioners, and shall not be absolutely allowed and confirmed, it shall be lawful for such commissioner or commissioners (upon proof before him or them, of any such vexatious defence as aforesaid having been made by the bankrupt) by a warrant in writing under his or their hand and seal, or hands and seals, directed to the officer or officers with whom such incomplete certificate shall then be remaining, to order such officer or officers to stay the certificate for such period as the commissioner or commissioners shall think fit, so as such period shall not exceed the term of         years, nor be less than         months, from the date of such warrant, and the officer or officers to whom such warrant shall be directed, shall thereupon retain the certificate until the expiration of the period in such warrant limited, and such certificate shall be of no effect from the granting of such warrant, till the expiration of such period.

XIV. AND be it enacted, That notwithstanding anything in this Act contained, *the payment or satisfaction of the debt and costs*, in any action wherein an averment of merits shall have been filed vexatiously, and without reasonable or probable cause, shall be and *be considered an extinguishment of the offence* of making such vexatious defence, except such payment or satisfaction shall appear to have been made with an intention to avoid the penalties of this Act.

XV. THAT after the defendant's default in pleading or appearing on the hearing or trial of any issue in law or fact, any *one of the judges* of the courts of Westminster, upon adequate cause shewn, *shall have power to order* that *no suggestion*, as in the 13th section mentioned, *shall be entered on the roll;* or if the same shall have been entered, to order that such suggestion shall be suppressed. Provided nevertheless, that after the expiration of six months from the entry of such judgment by default, the application for the omission or suppression of the suggestion of default on the roll, shall be made to the court in banc, in which the action was commenced.

XVI. THAT where a defendant shall admit part of the plaintiff's demand, and, at the proper stage of the action, shall pay such part thereof into court, an averment of merits previously made by him as to the whole demand, shall not be considered vexatious as to the part of the demand so paid into court, and nothing in this Act contained shall alter the law or practice of the courts at Westminster as to costs in cases of a tender or offer of part payment.

XVII. THAT the declaration in the proceedings under the writ of summons given by this Act, shall not omit any of the defendants named in such writ; and no defendant shall plead in abatement to such declaration for non-joinder of parties, unless within ten days after service of the writ, inclusive of the day of service, he shall appear to the writ, and file in addition to, or in lieu of an averment of merits, a notice signed by him, and witnessed by an attorney of one of the said courts, or otherwise signed by the defendant's attorney in the action, setting forth the objections to such writ, and the names and places of abode of the person or persons who may have been omitted to have been joined, which notice, as to the truth of the statements therein contained, shall be verified by affidavit, but a defendant in such case shall not be at liberty to plead, otherwise than in abatement, unless he shall have also filed an averment of merits.

XVIII. THAT, if in an action against two or more defendants, one or more should appear and file the averment of merits by this act required, and the other or others of them should neglect so to do, then upon affidavit of the service of the writ of summons and particulars of demand, and demand of appearance, on the defendant or defendants so neglecting to appear, the plaintiff shall be at liberty to enter an appearance for such defendant or defendants, and to proceed in the action according to the present practice; but the defendant or defendants so neglecting to appear, and to file such averment, shall be precluded from pleading to such action, unless the plaintiff, or his attorney, shall consent to receive a plea, or unless a judge, upon cause shewn and such averment subsequently filed, shall otherwise order.

XIX. That an office copy, certified by the officer with whom the original shall be filed, shall be sufficient evidence of any original document filed under the authority of this Act, in all courts of law and equity, unless the genuineness of such original document shall be disputed, and due notice that the genuineness thereof is disputed shall have been given by the party disputing the same, in which case, if the genuineness of such document be established, the party disputing the same shall in any event pay the cost of the production of the original.

XX. That nothing in this Act contained shall alter the present practice of the said courts under the writ of capias, given by an Act passed in the second and third year of the reign of his present Majesty, entitled, " An Act for the uniformity of process in personal actions in his Majesty's Courts of Law at Westminster;" and all provisions of the last named Act in any way relating to writs issued under the authority thereof, and particularly as to proceedings to outlawry, shall extend to and be applicable to writs issued under the authority of this present Act, except where the same are inconsistent with the terms of this present Act.

XXI. That the defendant shall be at liberty, before any judgment signed under the authority of this Act, to refer the costs claimed to be taxed by the proper officer, notwithstanding he may have confessed such costs under the provisions aforesaid, and, in case one equal sixth part thereof shall be disallowed, the plaintiff shall pay the costs of taxation, but in case one equal sixth part thereof shall not be disallowed, then such costs of taxation shall be paid by the defendant.

XXII. That it shall be lawful for the judges of the said courts, and they are hereby required to make all such general rules and orders for the effectual execution of this act, of the intention and object thereof, and for fixing the costs to be allowed for and in respect of the matters herein contained, and the performance thereof, and also the fees to be taken by the officers of the courts, as in their judgment, shall be deemed necessary and proper.

XXIII. That wherever this Act in describing or referring to the plaintiff or defendant, uses the word importing the singular number or the masculine gender only, the same shall be understood to include and shall be applied to several persons as well as one person, and females as well as males, and bodies corporate as well as individuals, unless there be something in the subject or context repugnant to such construction.

XXIV. That this Act shall commence and take effect, &c.

may be altered, &c. during the present session.

# SCHEDULE.

### No. 1.

WILLIAM THE FOURTH, &c. to C. D. of, &c. Greeting: We command you, [*or*, " as before," *or*, " often before We have commanded you,"] that within ten days after the service of this writ, inclusive of the day of such service, you do cause an appearance to be entered for you in Our court of
in an action on promises (*as the case may be*) at the suit of A. B.; nevertheless having regard to the notice hereunder written. Witness, &c.
at Westminster, the day of 1835.

N.B. *This writ is to be served within four calendar months from the date thereof, including the day of such date, and not afterwards.*

### A WARNING TO THE DEFENDANT.

TAKE NOTICE, that the plaintiff claims of you a debt of £          [*if the debt is one bearing interest, say here* " together with interest from the          day of          ,"] the particulars of which will be delivered to you on the service of this writ: And take notice, that IF YOU DENY THE said DEBT, and intend to defend the action, then you are by your attorney to cause an appearance to be entered to the writ, within ten days after service thereof, inclusive of the day of service; and at the time of so entering an appearance, you are likewise to cause to be entered a declaration in writing, to be signed by you, that you believe that you have good grounds of defence to the said action; but hereby TAKE WARNING, that if you so cause an appearance to be entered and make such declaration that you have a good defence, without having reasonable and probable grounds for denying the said debt, your so doing will be deemed vexatious, and in such case you will render yourself liable in certain events to imprisonment or other penalties: And further TAKE NOTICE, that IF YOU have no reasonable ground for defending the action, and ADMIT THE DEBT to be a just debt, then within the time allowed you as aforesaid for appearing hereto, you may pay the said debt, and £        for costs, to the plaintiff, his attorney or agent, and further proceedings will be stayed; or if you are not able to pay the same within such time, you may, by your attorney, enter a confession of the said debt, and submit to pay the same, and the costs aforesaid, within thirty-one days from the service hereof, and thereupon the proceedings against you will be stayed until the end of the said thirty-one days; and further TAKE NOTICE, that in case YOU NEGLECT to appear and defend, or to confess this action, then you will be deemed to have admitted the debt, and the plaintiff will be at liberty (after giving you a certain other notice) to sign judgment for the said debt and the costs of the action, and forthwith to take out execution against you.

---

No. 2.

In the

BETWEEN - - -        *Plaintiff*,
                and
                     *Defendant*.

WHEREAS, you have disregarded the writ of summons served on you, on the     day of     last [*or*, instant] in this action, wherein the plaintiff claims of you £     for debt, [*if the debt be one which bears interest, say here* " together with interest thereon, from the     day of     ."] Now, therefore, again TAKE NOTICE that, IF YOU DENY THE said DEBT, and intend to defend the action, then you are, by your attorney, to cause an appearance to be entered to the writ, within eight days after the service of this notice, inclusive of the day of service, and at the time of so entering an appearance, you are likewise to cause to be entered a declaration in writing, to be signed by you, that you believe you have good grounds of defence to the said action; but hereby TAKE WARNING that, if you do cause an appearance to be entered, and make such declaration that you have a good defence, without having reasonable and probable grounds for denying the said debt, your so doing will be deemed vexatious; and, in such case, you will, in certain events, render yourself liable to imprisonment and other penalties: and further, TAKE NOTICE that, IF YOU have no reasonable ground for defending the action, but ADMIT THE DEBT to be a just debt, then, within the time allowed you, as aforesaid, for appearing, you may pay the said debt, and £     for the costs of the said writ, and of this notice, making together £    , to the plaintiff, his attorney, or agent; and then further proceedings will be stayed;* or, if you are not able to pay the same within such time, you may, by your attorney, enter a confession of the said debt, and submit to pay the same, and the costs aforesaid, within thirty-one days † from the day of the service of the said writ of summons; and thereupon, all proceedings against you will be stayed, until the end of the said thirty-one days :* and further TAKE NOTICE that, IN CASE YOU NEGLECT to appear and defend,* or to confess this action,* then you will be deemed to have admitted the debt; and the plaintiff, after eight days from the service of this notice, will sign judgment, and forthwith take out execution against you. Dated this    of    , 1835.

To Mr. C. D., the above }    J. S.,
named defendant.    the plaintiff's attorney, or agent.

[† *If thirty-one days shall have expired, omit the words between the asterisks.*]

---

No. 3.

In the

BETWEEN - - -    *Plaintiff*,
and
*Defendant.*

I, C. D., of, &c., the defendant, [*or* "one of the defendants,"] above named [*or if by the attorney of such defendant*, "I, J. S., the attorney of C. D." &c.] do aver that I do not, [*or* "that the said C. D. doth not,"] owe to the plaintiff the sum of £.    , claimed in this action; and I declare that I believe I have [*or* "the said C. D." hath] good grounds of defence to the said action on the merits

C. D.
[*or* J. S., attorney of the above named defendant C. D.]

Witness to the signing hereof
by the above named defendant,
    J. S.
Defendant's attorney (or agent).

[*No attestation if the averment is signed by the defendant's attorney.*]

*If the defendant cannot write, and makes his mark, the form of attestation to be thus :*—" I, the undersigned, witnessed the signing of this averment, by the said C. D., the above-named defendant, the same having been previously read over and explained by me to him; and I certify to the court my belief that the said C. D. hath good grounds of defence to this action, and that his averment is true."

J. S.
Defendant's attorney (or agent.)

## No. 4.

In the

BETWEEN - - - *Plaintiff*,
and
*Defendant.*

I confess the debt of £ ; for goods sold and delivered by the plaintiff to me, [*or as the case may be, stating concisely the nature of the debt,*] which debt is claimed by the plaintiff's writ of summons, served on me on the day of , and I submit to pay the same, together with lawful interest thereon, from the date of the said writ, [*or if the debt be one that bears interest, say* " from the day of ," *according to the fact and statement in the writ,*] and also with £ for the costs claimed by the said writ, [*or* " demand of appearance,"] within thirty-one days from the said service of the said writ, further proceedings being in the mean time stayed; and in case I make default in paying the debt, interest, and costs as aforesaid, judgment shall be signed and execution issue against me, and the said debt and costs, with costs of judgment and execution, sheriff's charges, and other expences, shall be levied. Dated, &c.

C. D.

**Witness** to signing hereof by
the above named defendant,

J. S., of, &c.
Attorney (or agent) for the defendant.

---

## No. 5.

WILLIAM THE FOURTH, &c. To the Sheriff of greeting: We command you that you omit not by reason of any liberty in your bailiwick, but that you enter the same, and distrain upon the goods and chattels of C. D. for the sum of forty shillings, in order to compel his appearance in Our court of to answer A. B. in a plea of promises [*or as the case may be*], and how you shall execute this writ make known to Us in Our said court on the day of now next ensuing. Witness, &c.

*Notice to be subscribed to the foregoing writ.*—Mr. C. D., Take notice, that I have this day distrained upon your goods and chattels in the sum of forty shillings, in consequence of your not having appeared in the said court to answer to the said A. B., according to the exigency of a writ of summons, bearing teste on the      day of          whereby the said plaintiff claims of you, £      for a debt [*if the debt be one bearing interest, say here,* " together with interest from the      day of      183  , *as in the writ of summons,*] the particulars of which have been delivered to you, and take notice, &c. &c. [*as in the warning to the writ of summons, except that for the time of appearing, limit eight days inclusive from the return of the distringas, and instead of fixing an amount of costs, say,* " costs to be taxed," *and instead of the words,* "after giving you a certain other notice," *say,* " to apply to a judge for leave," &c.]

---

### No. 6.

The    day of      in the      year of the reign of King William the Fourth.

[The County where defendant resides] TO WIT. } Whereas C. D. of, &c., was served on the    day of    with a writ of summons at the suit of A. B., whereby the said A. B. claimed of the said C. D. a debt of £    for goods sold and delivered by the said A. B. to the said C. D. [*or as the case may be, and if the debt be one bearing interest, say,* " together with interest thereon from the    day of    ," *as expressed in the writ*], and an appearance was duly demanded on the    day of    as by the said writ of summons and affidavits filed of record in this court doth appear. Wherefore the said defendant not having appeared to the said writ or entered a confession of the said debt, It is considered that the said A. B. do recover against the said C. D. the debt [and interest] aforesaid, to £    , and also £    for his costs and charges by the court here adjudged.

Let execution issue
for £    debt,
and    costs.

---

£    besides, &c.
P. Q.

No. 7.

The     day of     in the year of the reign of King William the Fourth.

[The county of defendant's residence.]
TO WIT.
} Whereas, C. D., of, &c. was served on the     day of     with a writ of summons at the suit of A. B., whereby the said A. B. claimed of the said C. D. a debt of £     for goods sold and delivered by the said A. B. to the said C. D. [*or as the case may be.*] and whereas the said C. D. has filed in this court a confession, whereby he hath confessed the said debt, and submitted to pay the same with interest thereon, from     and the costs and charges of the plaintiff to £     within thirty-one days from the said service of the writ. Wherefore the said C. D. having made default therein, It is considered that the said A. B. do recover against the said C. D. the said debt, interest, and costs, as aforesaid, to £     and also £     for further costs and charges, by the court here adjudged, which said debt and costs amount, in the whole, to £

Let execution issue
   for £     debt, interest, and
                 costs confessed,
   and £     costs of judgment.
   ―――
   £     besides, &c.
         P. Q.

No. 8.

The     day of     in     Term in the     year of the reign of his Majesty King William the Fourth.

[The County where defendant resides]
TO WIT.
} Whereas C. D., of, &c., having had notice of a writ of summons at the suit of A. B., whereby the said A. B. claimed of the said C. D. a debt of £     for goods sold and delivered, &c. [*as the case may be, and if the debt be one bearing interest, add* " with interest thereon from the     day of     ," *as in the writ,*] and the said C. D. not having appeared thereto, a writ of distringas returnable on the     day of

By order of Mr. Justice dated

having thereupon issued, and forty shillings having been levied of the goods and chattels of the said C. D. and the said C. D. having made further default, It is considered that the said A. B. do recover against the said C. D. the said debt [and interest] to £      together with £      for costs and charges by the court here adjudged to the said A. B.

Let execution issue for
£      debt and
£      costs.
———
£      besides, &c.
  P Q.

Printed by Libri Plureos GmbH in Hamburg, Germany